W9-CDE-112

This book has been
withdrawn from the
St. Joseph County Public Library
due to

_____ deteriorated/defective condition
_____ obsolete information
_____ superceded by newer holdings
_____ excess copies reduced demand
_____ other _____

4-55 ___ Date _____ Staff

# THE EENTSY, WEENTSY SPIDER

## FINGERPLAYS AND ACTION RHYMES

COMPILED BY

## JOANNA COLE

AND

## STEPHANIE CALMENSON

ILLUSTRATED BY

## ALAN TIEGREEN

Morrow Junior Books / New York

PUBLIC LIBRARY
JAN 16 1992
SOUTH BEND, INDIANA

LA SALLE BRANCH LIBRARY
3232 W. ARDMORE TRAIL
SOUTH BEND, INDIANA 46628

# TO JOSHUA AND ZACHARY DANNETT

For their help in researching this book, thanks to Celia Holm, Children's Librarian at the Donnell Library in New York City, and to Mrs. "Mike" Vuillemenot and her staff at the Cyrenius H. Booth Library Children's Room in Newtown, Connecticut.

Text copyright © 1991 by Joanna Cole and Stephanie Calmenson
Illustrations copyright © 1991 by Alan Tiegreen
All rights reserved.
No part of this book may be reproduced or utilized
in any form or by any means, electronic or mechanical,
including photocopying, recording or by any information storage and retrieval system,
without permission in writing from the Publisher.
Inquiries should be addressed to
William Morrow and Company, Inc.,
1350 Avenue of the Americas, New York, NY 10019.
Printed in the United States of America.
1  2  3  4  5  6  7  8  9  10
Library of Congress Cataloging-in-Publication Data
Cole, Joanna.
The eentsy, weentsy spider : fingerplays and action rhymes/
compiled by Joanna Cole and Stephanie Calmenson; illustrated by
Alan Tiegreen.
p.   cm.
Includes index.
Summary: A collection of play rhymes intended to be accompanied by
finger play and other physical activities.
ISBN 0-688-09438-4—ISBN 0-688-09439-2 (library).
1. Finger play—Juvenile literature.   2. Rhyming games—Juvenile
literature.   [1. Finger play.]   I. Calmenson, Stephanie.
II. Tiegreen, Alan, ill.   III. Title.
GV1218.F5C62  1991
793.4—dc20     90-44594     CIP     AC

793.4 C675e          LAS
Cole, Joanna.
The eentsy, weentsy spider

# CONTENTS

# FINGERPLAYS AND ACTION RHYMES

Fingerplays and action rhymes, like nursery rhymes, have been kept alive for generations because children love them. The musical language of the rhymes makes them easy to say and remember. The actions, too, are perfect for children, who love to participate. It's fun to make the tickly little steps of "The Eentsy, Weentsy Spider" climbing up the waterspout, to pretend to pound in a nail while singing "The Hammer Song," and to tip over your whole body for "I'm a Little Teapot."

Many of the rhymes reflect a child's world. They are about mealtime and bedtime and families. They are about the natural phenomena a child sees every day—rain, flowers, animals large and small. And they give children an opportunity to learn about left and right, up and down, and their bodies from head to toe.

So say them, sing them—there are musical arrangements at the back of the book—act them out. They really are fun!

# TEN LITTLE FIREFIGHTERS

Ten little firefighters
Sleeping in a row.

Ding, ding goes the bell,

And down the pole they go.

Off on the engine, oh, oh, oh.

Using the big hose, so, so, so.

When all the fire's out, home so slow.

Back into bed, all in a row.

# BALLOONS

This is the way
We blow our balloon.

Blow!

Blow!

Blow!

This is the way
We break our balloon.

Oh, oh, no!

— 8 —

# TWO FAT SAUSAGES

Two fat sausages

Sizzling in the pan.

One went POP!

*Pop!*

The other went BAM!

# SIX LITTLE DUCKS

Six little ducks
That I once knew.

WIGGLE
FINGERS

Fat ducks, skinny ducks,
Fair ducks, too.

But the one little duck
With a feather on his back,

He led the others with
A quack, quack, quack.

Down to the river
They would go,
Wibble-wobble, wibble-wobble,
To and fro.

But the one little duck
With a feather on his back,

He led the others with a quack, quack, quack!
Quack, quack, quack. Quack, quack, quack.
He led the others with a quack, quack, quack!

# OPEN, SHUT THEM

Open,
Shut them.

Open,
Shut them.

Give a little clap.

Open,
Shut them.

Open,
Shut them.

Place them in your lap.

— 12 —

Creep them, creep them.
Creep them, creep them

Right up to your chin.
Open wide your little mouth,

But do not let them in.

# RAIN

Drum
fingers
on
floor

Pitter-pat, pitter-pat,
The rain goes on for hours.
And though it keeps me in the house,

It's very          good for          flowers.

# APPLES

Way up high in the apple tree,

Two little apples smiled at me.

shake arms

I shook that tree as hard as I could.

Drop hands to lap

Down came the apples—
Mmm, were they good!

# TEN LITTLE FINGERS

I have ten little fingers,
And they all belong to me.
I can make them do things.
Would you like to see?

I can shut them up tight

Or open them wide.

I can put them together

Or make them all hide.

I can make them jump high

Or make them go low.

I can fold them up quietly
And sit just so.

# THE QUIET MOUSE

Once there lived a quiet mouse    In a quiet little house.
When all was quiet as can be,

OUT POPPED HE!

# GRANDMA'S SPECTACLES

Here are Grandma's spectacles,

And here is Grandma's hat;

And here's the way she folds her hands
And puts them in her lap.

# I'M A LITTLE TEAPOT

I'm a little teapot,
Short and stout.

Here is my handle.

Here is my spout.

When I get all steamed up,
Hear me shout,
"Tip me over and pour me out!"

# ☕ HERE'S A CUP ☕

Here's a cup,

And here's a cup,

And here's a pot of tea.

Pour a cup,

And pour a cup,

And have a drink with me.

# BLUEBIRDS

Two little bluebirds
Sitting on a hill,

One named Jack,

The other named Jill.

Fly away, Jack.

Fly away, Jill.

Come back, Jack.

Come back, Jill.

# GREAT BIG BALL

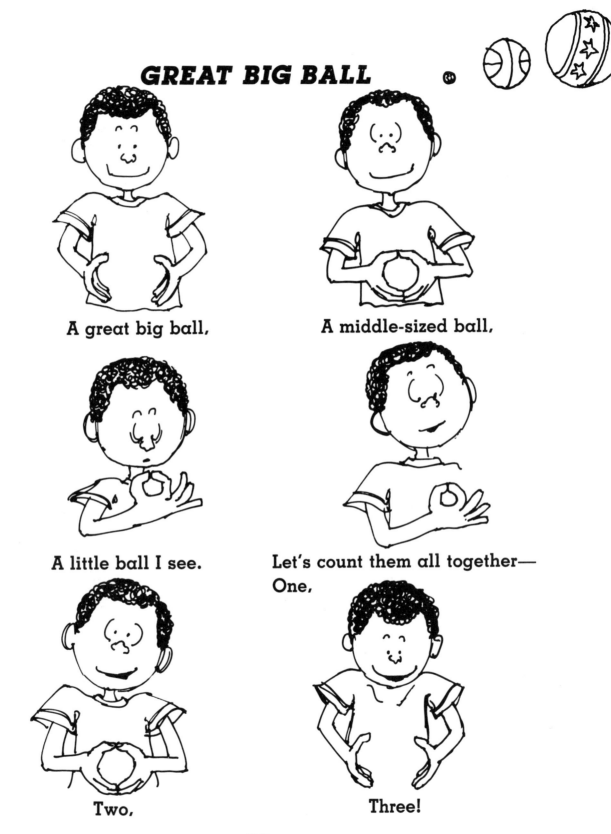

A great big ball,

A middle-sized ball,

A little ball I see.

Let's count them all together—
One,

Two,

Three!

# MY HAT

My hat it has three corners,

Three corners has my hat.

If it did not have three corners,

It would not be my hat.

 # THE EENTSY, WEENTSY SPIDER

ARMS GO UP
AS FINGERS
"CLIMB"

The eentsy, weentsy spider
Climbed up the waterspout.

Down came the rain

And washed the spider out.

Out came the sun

And dried up all the rain.

And the eentsy, weentsy spider
Climbed up the spout again.

# UP TO THE CEILING

Up to the ceiling,

Down to the floor.

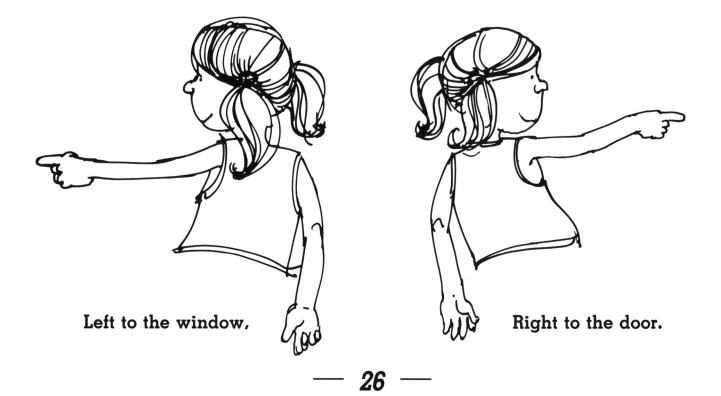

Left to the window,

Right to the door.

This is my right hand—
Raise it up high.

This is my left hand—
Reach for the sky.

Twirl
hands

Right hand, left hand,
Twirl them around.

Left hand, right hand,
Pound, pound, pound.

 # HERE IS THE CHURCH

Here is the church.

Here is the steeple.

Open the doors

And see all the people.

# HERE ARE MOTHER'S KNIVES AND FORKS

Here are Mother's knives and forks.

Here is Grandma's table.

Here is Sister's looking glass.

Rock Cradle

And here is Baby's cradle.

# THE HAMMER SONG

Jenny works with one hammer,
One hammer, one hammer.
Jenny works with one hammer.
Then she works with two.

Jenny works with two hammers,
Two hammers, two hammers.
Jenny works with two hammers.
Then she works with three.

Jenny works with three hammers,
Three hammers, three hammers.
Jenny works with three hammers.
Then she works with four.

Jenny works with four hammers,
Four hammers, four hammers.
Jenny works with four hammers.
Then she works with five.

Jenny works with five hammers,
Five hammers, five hammers.
Jenny works with five hammers . . .

**Then she goes to sleep!**

# MY TURTLE

This is my turtle.
He lives in a shell.
He likes his home very well.

He pokes his head out
When he wants to eat.

And he pulls it back
When he wants to sleep.

# FIVE LITTLE KITTENS

Five little kittens
Standing in a row,

They nod their heads
To the children, so.

They run to the left,
They run to the right,

They stand up and stretch
In the bright sunlight.

Along comes a dog,
Who's in for some fun.

Meow! See those
Five kittens run.

# THE WHEELS ON THE BUS

The wheels on the bus
Go round and round,
Round and round,
Round and round.
The wheels on the bus
Go round and round
All over town!

Twirl
hands

The driver on the bus
Goes "Move to the rear!
Move to the rear!
Move to the rear!"
The driver on the bus
Goes "Move to the rear!"
All over town!

**The people on the bus**
**Go up and down,**
(and so on)

**The babies on the bus**
**Go "Wah! Wah! Wah!"**
(and so on)

**The mothers on the bus**
**Go "Shh, shh, shh,"**
(and so on)

(You can add other verses, too. Try "money goes
clink," "wipers go swish," and "children go yakkity-yak.")

# WHERE IS THUMBKIN?

**Where is Thumbkin?**
**Where is Thumbkin?**    Here I am!    Here I am!

How are you today, sir?

Very well, I thank you.

Run away,

Run away.

(Repeat with all the fingers: Pointer, Tall Man,
Ring Man, and Pinkie.)

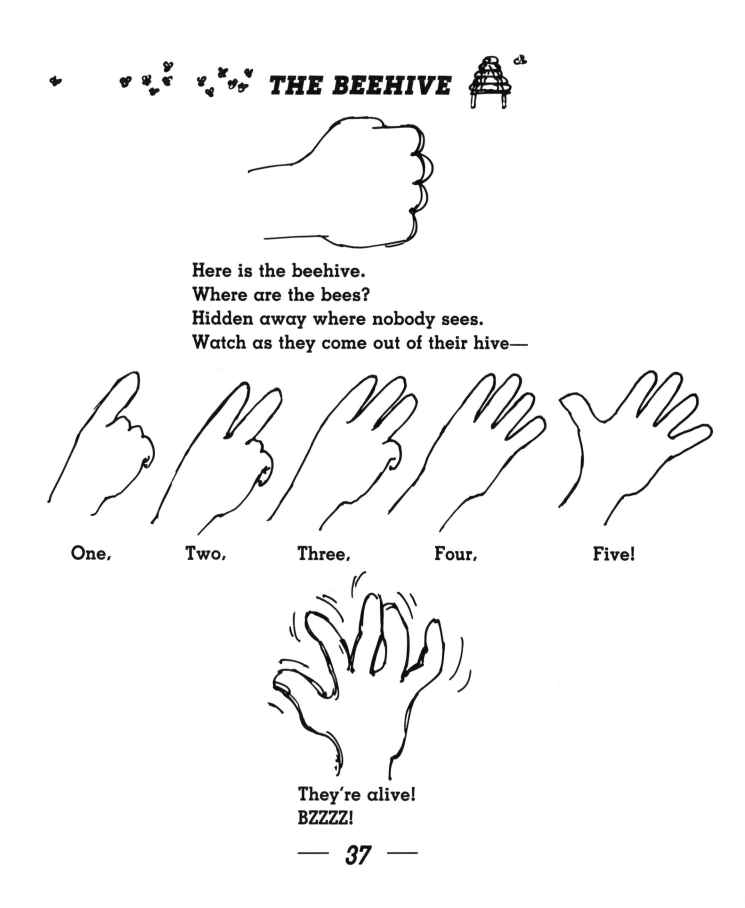

# THE BEEHIVE

Here is the beehive.
Where are the bees?
Hidden away where nobody sees.
Watch as they come out of their hive—

One,    Two,    Three,    Four,    Five!

They're alive!
BZZZZ!

# FIVE LITTLE MONKEYS

Five little monkeys
Jumping on the bed.

One fell off
And bumped his head.

Mama called the doctor,
And the doctor said,

"That's what you get
For jumping on the bed!"

shake finger

**Four little monkeys . . .**
(and so on)

**Three little monkeys . . .**
(and so on)

**Two little monkeys . . .**
(and so on)

**One little monkey**
**Jumping on the bed.**
**He fell off**
**And bumped his head.**
**Mama called the doctor,**
**And the doctor said,**
**"No more monkeys**
**Jumping on the bed!"**

 # TEN FAT PEAS

Ten fat peas in a peapod pressed.

One grew. . . . Two grew.    So did all the rest.

They grew and grew    And did not stop    Until one day
The pod went POP!

# THE GRASSHOPPER

**There was a little grasshopper**

**Who was always on the jump.**

**And because he never looked ahead,
He always got a bump.**

# IF YOU'RE HAPPY AND YOU KNOW IT

CLAP
TWICE
AFTER
SINGING
WORDS

CLAP
TWICE

If you're happy and you know it,
Clap your hands.

If you're happy and you know it,
Clap your hands.

CLAP
TWICE

If you're happy and you know it,
And you really want to show it,
If you're happy and you know it,
Clap your hands.

(Continue with other actions, such as stamp your
feet, touch your knees, nod your head, say
"Achoo!")

# THE PEANUT SONG

Oh, a peanut sat
On a railroad track,

His heart was all a-flutter.

Along came the five-fifteen,

Uh-oh, peanut butter!

# WHOOPS, JOHNNY!

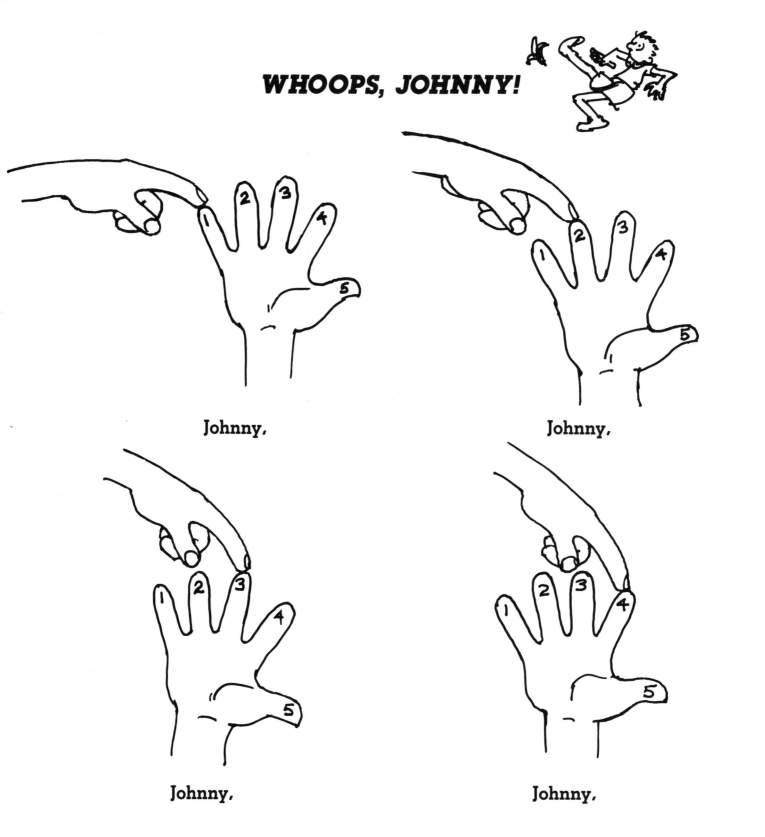

Johnny,

Johnny,

Johnny,

Johnny,

— 44 —

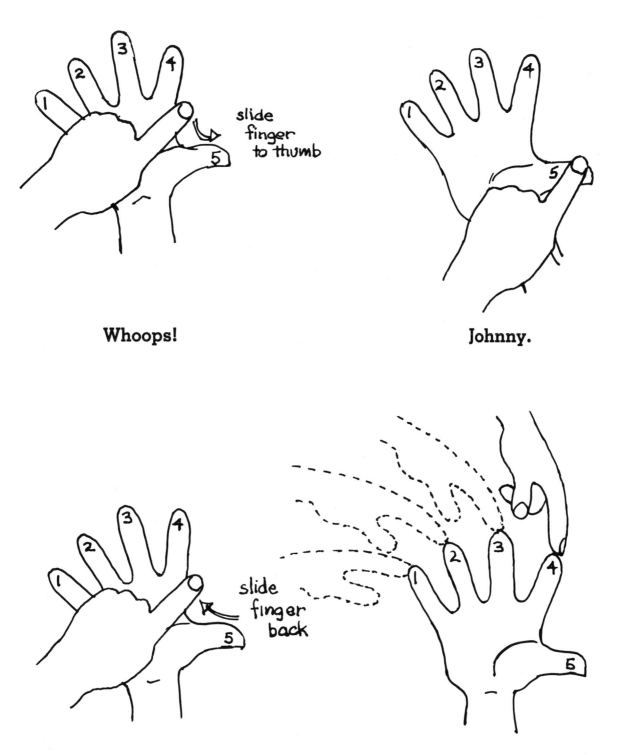

slide
finger
to thumb

**Whoops!**

**Johnny.**

slide
finger
back

**Whoops!**

**Johnny, Johnny, Johnny, Johnny.**

# THIS OLD MAN

Tap thumbs together

Tap Knees

This old man, he played one.

He played knick-knack
On his thumb.

With a knick-knack,

Clap! Clap!

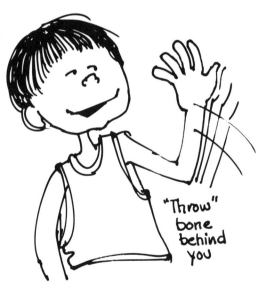

"Throw" bone behind you

Twirl hands

Paddy-whack,

Give your dog a bone.

This old man came
Rolling home.

**2nd Verse:**

**This old man, he played two.**
**He played knick-knack**
**On his shoe.**
(and so on)

**3rd Verse:** "three" . . . "knee"

**4th Verse:** "four" . . . "door"

**5th Verse:** "five" . . . "hive"

**6th Verse:** "six" . . . "sticks"

**7th Verse:** "seven" . . . "up to heaven"

**8th Verse:** "eight" . . . "gate"

**9th Verse:** "nine" . . . "spine"

**10th Verse:** "ten" . . . "once again"

TOUCH SHOE

TOUCH KNEE

PRETEND TO KNOCK

TAP FIST

TAP INDEX FINGERS TOGETHER

POINT UP

TAP HAND

TAP SPINE

CLAP HANDS

# TWO FAT GENTLEMEN

**Two fat gentlemen**
**Met in a glen,**

**Bowed most politely,**
**Bowed once again.**

**How do you do? How do you do?**
**And how do you do again?**

(Repeat with "two thin ladies" [index fingers]; "two tall policemen" [middle fingers]; "two happy schoolchildren" [ring fingers]; "two little babies" [pinkies].)

# CHOOK-CHOOK-CHOOK

Chook, chook, chook-chook-chook.
Good morning, Mrs. Hen.
How many children have you got?
Madam, I've got ten.

Four of them
Are yellow,

And four of them
Are brown,

And two of them
Are speckled red—
The nicest in the town!

# THE ELEPHANT

The elephant goes like this and that.

He's oh, so big,
And he's oh, so fat.

He has no fingers,
And he has no toes,

But goodness gracious,
What a nose!

# BIRTHDAY CAKE

Ten candles on a birthday cake,

All lit up for me.

I'll make a wish and blow them out.

Blow and
bend fingers
down

Watch and you will see.
*Whhh!*

# ON MY HEAD

On my head my hands I place.

On my shoulders,

On my face,

On my hips,

And at my side,

**Then behind me they will hide.**

**I will hold them up so high,
Quickly make my fingers fly,**

**Hold them out in front of me,**

clap!
clap!
clap!

**Swiftly clap them—
One, two, three.**

 **TEN IN THE BED**

There were ten in the bed,

And the little one said,
"Roll over! Roll over!"

So they all rolled over,
And one fell out.

There were nine in the bed,
(and so on)

There were eight in the bed. . . .

There were seven in the bed. . . .

There were six in the bed. . . .

There were five in the bed. . . .

There were four in the bed. . . .

There were three in the bed. . . .

There were two in the bed. . . .

There was one in the bed,
And the little one said,
"Good night!"

# MUSICAL ARRANGEMENTS

## SIX LITTLE DUCKS
(see pages 10-11)

Six lit - tle ducks That I once knew. Fat ducks, skin-ny ducks,
Down to the riv - er They would go, Wib-ble-wob-ble, wib-ble-wob-ble,

Fair ducks, too.} But the one lit - tle duck With a feath-er on his back,
To and fro.

He led the oth-ers with a quack, quack, quack. Quack, quack, quack.

Quack, quack, quack. He led the oth-ers with a quack, quack, quack!

# OPEN, SHUT THEM

(see pages 12-13)

O - pen, Shut them. O - pen, Shut them. Give a lit - tle clap.

O - pen, Shut them. O - pen, Shut them. Place them in your lap.

Creep them, creep them. Creep them, creep them Right up to your chin.

O - pen wide your lit - tle mouth, But do not let them in.

# I'M A LITTLE TEAPOT

(see page 20)

I'm a lit - tle tea - pot, Short and stout.

Here is my han - dle, Here is my spout. When I get all steamed up,

Hear me shout, "Tip me o - ver and pour me out!"

# BLUEBIRDS
(see page 22)

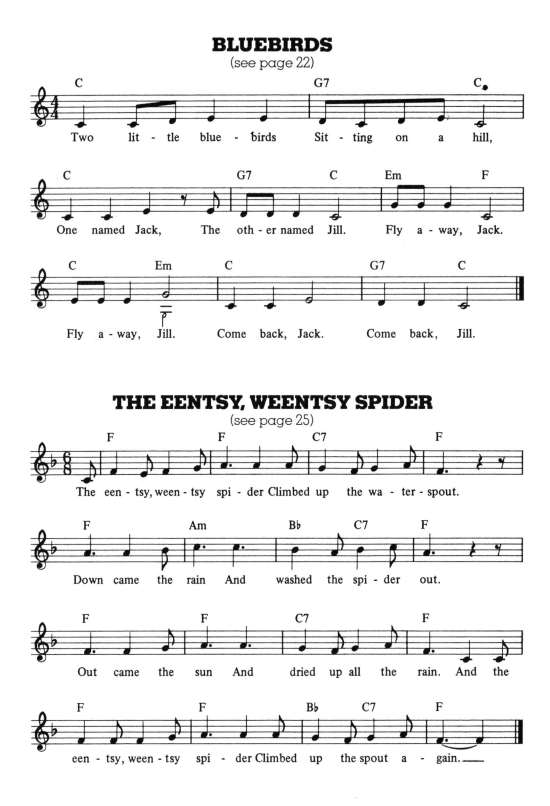

Two lit - tle blue - birds Sit - ting on a hill,

One named Jack, The oth - er named Jill. Fly a - way, Jack.

Fly a - way, Jill. Come back, Jack. Come back, Jill.

# THE EENTSY, WEENTSY SPIDER
(see page 25)

The een - tsy, ween - tsy spi - der Climbed up the wa - ter - spout.

Down came the rain And washed the spi - der out.

Out came the sun And dried up all the rain. And the

een - tsy, ween - tsy spi - der Climbed up the spout a - gain.

# THE HAMMER SONG
(see pages 30-31)

1. Jen - ny works with one ham - mer, One ham - mer,
one ham - mer. Jen - ny works with one ham - mer.

**1.2.3.4.**
Then she works with two.

**5.**
Then she goes to sleep!

2. Jenny works with two hammers, Two hammers, two hammers.
Jenny works with two hammers. Then she works with three.

3. Jenny works with three hammers, Three hammers, three hammers.
Jenny works with three hammers. Then she works with four.

4. Jenny works with four hammers, Four hammers, four hammers.
Jenny works with four hammers. Then she works with five.

5. Jenny works with five hammers, Five hammers, five hammers.
Jenny works with five hammers. Then she goes to sleep!

# THE WHEELS ON THE BUS
(see pages 34-35)

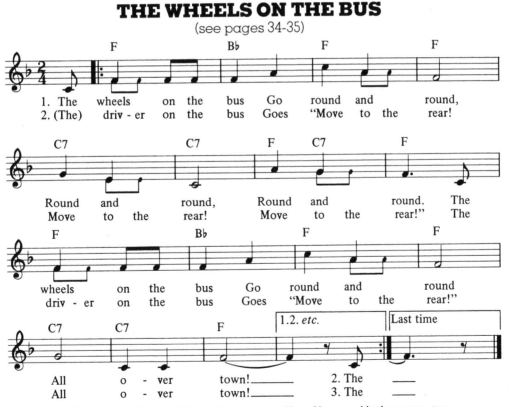

1. The wheels on the bus Go round and round,
2. (The) driv - er on the bus Goes "Move to the rear!

Round and round, Round and round. The
Move to the rear! Move to the rear!" The

wheels on the bus Go round and round
driv - er on the bus Goes "Move to the rear!"

**1.2. etc.**
All o - ver town!_____ 2. The _____
All o - ver town!_____ 3. The _____

**Last time**

3. The people on the bus Go up and down, (etc.)
4. The babies on the bus Go "Wah! Wah! Wah!" (etc.)
5. The mothers on the bus Go "Shh, shh, shh," (etc.)

Note: You can add other verses, too.
Try, "money goes clink," "wipers go swish,"
and "children go yakkity-yak."

# WHERE IS THUMBKIN?

(see page 36)

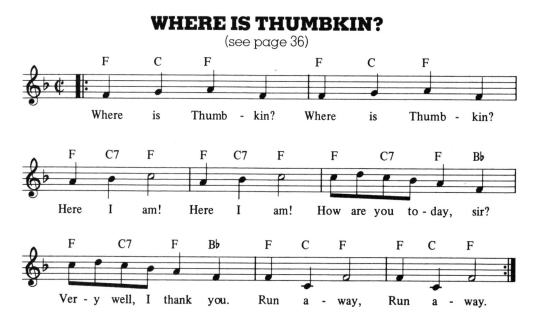

(Repeat with all the fingers: Pointer, Tall Man, Ring Man, and Pinkie.)

# IF YOU'RE HAPPY AND YOU KNOW IT

(see page 42)

(Continue with other actions, such as stamp your feet, nod your head, say "Achoo!")

# THE PEANUT SONG

(see page 43)

Oh, a pea - nut sat On a rail - road track, His heart was all a - flut - ter. A - long came the five - fif - teen, Uh - oh, pea - nut but - ter!

# THIS OLD MAN

(see pages 46-47)

1. This old man, he played one. He played knick - knack
2. This old man, he played two. He played knick - knack

On his thumb.}
On his shoe.} With a knick - knack, Pad - dy - whack,

Give your dog a bone. This old man came Roll - ing home.

ADDITIONAL VERSES:

3rd verse: "three" . . . "knee"      7th verse: "seven" . . . "up to heaven"
4th verse: "four" . . . "door"       8th verse: "eight" . . . "gate"
5th verse: "five" . . . "hive"       9th verse: "nine" . . . "spine"
6th verse: "six" . . . "sticks"      10th verse: "ten" . . . "once again"

# TEN IN THE BED

(see pages 54-55)

There were ten in the bed, And the lit-tle one said, "Roll

*(Repeat through "two in the bed,")*

o - ver! Roll o - ver!" So they all rolled o - ver, And

one fell out. There were nine* in the bed, And the

*(Repeat 7 times)*

lit - tle one said, "Roll o - ver! Roll o - ver!" So they

*(Last time only)*

all rolled o - ver, And one fell out. There was

one in the bed, And the lit - tle one said, *(spoken)* "Good night!"

*Eight in the bed, etc.
Continue until "two in the bed,"
then end with "Last time only" section.

# WHERE TO FIND MORE

## SOME SOURCES FOR FINGERPLAYS AND ACTION RHYMES

Brown, Marc. *Finger Rhymes.* New York: E. P. Dutton, 1980.

———. *Hand Rhymes.* New York: E. P. Dutton, 1985.

———. *Play Rhymes.* New York: E. P. Dutton, 1987.

Delamar, Gloria T. *Children's Counting-Out Rhymes, Fingerplays, Jump-Rope and Ball-Bounce Chants, and Other Rhythms.* Jefferson, N.C.: McFarland, 1983.

Emerson, Sally. *The Nursery Treasury.* New York: Doubleday, 1988.

Glazer, Tom. *Music for Ones and Twos.* Garden City, N.Y.: Doubleday, 1983.

———. *Eye Winker, Tom Tinker, Chin Chopper.* Garden City, N.Y.: Doubleday, 1973.

Grayson, Marion. *Let's Do Fingerplays.* Washington, D.C.: Robert B. Luce, 1962.

Hayes, Sarah. *Clap Your Hands.* New York: Lothrop, Lee & Shepard, 1988.

Jacobs, E. Frances. *Finger Plays and Action Rhymes.* New York: Lothrop, Lee and Shepard, 1941.

Matterson, Elizabeth. *Games for the Very Young.* New York: American Heritage Press, 1969.

Pooley, Sarah. *A Day of Rhymes.* New York: Alfred A. Knopf, 1987.

Poulsson, Emilie. *Finger Plays for Nursery and Kindergarten.* Boston: Lothrop, Lee and Shepard, 1893.

# INDEX OF FIRST LINES

j793.4 C675e          LAS
Cole, Joanna.
The eentsy, weentsy spider